SAINT
BUKO
WS
KI

(poems and stories by troy kody cunio)

SAINT BUKOWSKI

Saint Bukowski
Copyright © 2016 by Troy Kody Cunio
All rights reserved. This book or any portion thereof
may not be reproduced or used in any manner whatsoever
without the express written permission of the author
except for the use of brief quotations in a book review.
Printed in the United States of America

First Printing, 2016

ISBN-13: 978-1533311146
ISBN-10: 1533311145

(everything
 you need
   to know)

(more books)

citrusbeatpress@gmail.com
facebook.com/citrusbeatpress
tkcpoetry@gmail.com
payhip.com/tkcpoetry
tkcpoetry.webs.com
www.facebook.com/tkcpoetry

(this one is for Claire Frost)

(a better friend than anyone could ask for)

CONTENTS

The Outermost

Heartbreak Junkies

Juice

Kintsugi

Poetry Lessons

Someday I'll Love Troy Cunio

Speed

The Woman Whose Job It Was To Watch The Moon

[yeah.]

32 Bullet Points That Have Been Mistaken for a Handgun

When we are angels

[yeah.]

Lakeland Blues Traveler

If Books Could Kill

An Academic Poem

Botflies

Guate Nocturne

the boy or girl

The Outermost

Bet you couldn't tell, but
I'm a Russian nesting doll.

My navel opens to reveal
another Troy
just a bit smaller, older, sadder.

There are dozens of us.
We all live together under this skin.

There's a shriveled, fist-sized
Troy in the center of us all.
He makes most of the decisions.

Occasionally the outermost Troy
will peel himself off
and wander away.

We don't know what happens to them.
We like to think they're all still out there. Hollow,
looking for someone to fill their empty

Heartbreak Junkies

Again we crash, then we yearn
for the butterfly's rise when the burning fades.
We heartbreak junkies never learn

from the pasts we've hurt so hard to earn.
Like children digging up buried grenades,
again we clash. Then, we yearn.

Your kiss starts to sear like a cigarette burn
and my fingertips sharpen into switchblades.
We heartbreak junkies never learn.

Rebuilding bridges we tried to spurn,
exhuming togetherness long decayed,
we never last but still we yearn.

The ocean between us may toss and churn
and your laugh lines harden like barricades
but we heartbreak junkies never learn.

Smash the syringes, we'll still return
to a forever like a snowcap about to cascade.
Again we'll crash, then we'll yearn.
We heartbreak junkies never learn.

Juice

Even as a child, Marshall always suspected that something was wrong with Johnny. In Kindergarten, Johnny used to poke himself in the eye whenever he tried to pick his nose. In kickball, he could not make it from home plate to first base without stumbling halfway to the pitcher's mound and back. Marshall's earliest theory regarding Johnny's clumsiness was cooties, contracted when Johnny mistakenly gave himself the Blob Blob Slap Slap inoculation rather than the customary Circle Circle Dot Dot. This explanation eventually went the way of Santa Claus, but Johnny's strangeness did not.

Marshall eventually found that associating with Johnny carried a certain social cost. Homecoming was out of the question. Johnny's lack of sexual prowess was communicated between the girls of Andrew Jackson High in a secret language of stares, giggles, subtle hand gestures, and scrambled notes. It wasn't that he was ugly- he wasn't. As Marshall learned later, the issue was that for a teenage boy Johnny was not very excitable. In fact, he couldn't get excited even if he tried. As if that wasn't bad enough, he always gave off an aroma that was as unlikely as it was putrid - equal parts Germ-X and fermented armpit. Marshall was an intelligent, well groomed, and charismatic young man, but his stubborn friendship with Johnny kept him from enjoying anything more than a peripheral presence in the school's cliques. By their senior year, Marshall had no remaining close friendships with the upper social strata of the school.

Still, Marshall stuck out those difficult years. After all, Johnny had no one else to cover for him when, after a seemingly innocuous evening of video games and pizza, he insisted on commandeering his little sister's bicycle and riding it down the interstate off-ramp at 3 AM. He broke three teeth, his ulna, and both training wheels that night. Or there was the time when three cheerleaders decided that Johnny presented a unique challenge. They locked themselves in a handicapped stall with him and spent 45 minutes trying to elicit a biological response. It was Marshall who came to Johnny's rescue. Moral duty aside, Marshall liked Johnny. He told funny stories and and frequently told Marshall in his slurry drawl that he loved him and was so thankful to have a friend like him. Johnny was always good for borrowing lunch money or the newest Call of Duty. Best of all, he never told anyone when Marshall confessed his secrets to him, like that he frequented websites where women who should be enjoying happy retirements did unspeakable things with common household objects. It was like owning a clumsy puppy dog that no one else wanted. If he smelled a little and sometimes pissed on your backpack, so what?

    The true explanation for Johnny's strangeness came years later. On a warm spring evening, a Sheriff's Deputy pulled him over for swerving and going 25 over the limit. Johnny denied having been drinking despite failing a breathalyzer. He did pass the "walk in a straight line" test, albeit only on his hands and knees. The resulting court case was a textbook example of this country's justice system working as intended. The judge noticed that Johnny was visibly inebriated at a hearing despite having been in the company of his lawyer for three hours prior- the attorney claimed under oath that they had eaten lunch together, but Johnny had not consumed any alcohol. The judge ordered a thorough medical examination, which found that Johnny suffered from a rare condition- a rare kind of yeast living in his intestines turned any carbohydrate that he ate into alcohol, which then intoxicated the teetotalling Johnny. The honorable judge let Johnny off without fine or imprisonment, but his driver's license was revoked. Marshall, who was away at the State University working on an MBA, read about the case on the internet and everything fell into place. Johnny wasn't stupid, at least not at birth- God only knew what years of constant intoxication had done to his developing brain cells. And he wasn't a case of stunted sexual development, either- he just had perpetual whiskey dick.

    This was a tragedy, obviously, but it soon dawned on Marshall that it presented a unique business opportunity. Small amounts of liquor made from Johnny's piss could quite possibly turn a profit. It would be a niche market- the demand would come mostly from the obscurest, hippest, and most affluent corners of Asheville and Portland. But if it caught on, it could make millions. When Johnny heard the scheme, he trusted his old friend's business acumen. After a summer of experimentation they were able to fine tune Johnny's diet to produce urine that was exactly 31.5% ABV after distillation. Peaty with a smooth finish. With a twist of lime, it was exquisite.

    The friends decided to incorporate before taking their product to market. They would each be part owners, with Marshall taking 99% of the profit from their partnership. Johnny was of course drunk when he signed the contract. Understandably, the concoction- bottled as "Johnny's Juice: Small Batch Man Brewed Beverage "- got a lot of media attention, especially after Johnny appeared on

Shark Tank. Demand rose and before long Johnny's Juice was selling for $1000 per 40oz bottle. Marshall soon scored a contract with Bacardi to mass produce a non-piss based liquor under the Johnny's Juice brand. In the meantime he began cutting Johnny's Juice with lemonade and Absolut to help make up for the supply shortcomings of the real McCoy. Briefly, Marshall even considered selling eyedroppers filled with Johnny's semen, but that was quickly nixed. Like the cheerleaders, he couldn't solve the problem of production.

Meanwhile, erectile dysfunction was the least of Johnny's concerns. His belly became distended from the copious amounts of bread and Coca-Cola he had to consume to meet his quota. He took to wearing a bib to soak up the constant stream of drool that dripped from the sides of his mouth. Walking was a chore, and he frequently split his head open on tables and wall corners. Sometimes he would miss the distillery's collection trough when he urinated, setting him back on his daily volume goal. When he saw how much trouble Johnny had taking care of himself, Marshall moved him to the bottling facility full time. Johnny spent his days hooked up to a catheter, periodically texting Marshall poorly focused selfies and irrelevant cat memes.

One day Johnny's liver failed. He died having not been completely sober since being weaned from breast milk. Marshall was preparing to break the news to his investors when he got a call from a business partner. The research he had been funding in China had reached a breakthrough- it was now possible to induce Johnny's condition in human subjects. Street urchins were already being acquired for production purposes. Even the common man would soon be able to enjoy a cocktail made from authentic human urine.

Marshall opened a compartment in his desk. He withdrew a snifter and the last remaining bottle of the original Johnny's Juice. He poured himself a drink. Swirled it around gently, took in the faint flavor of ammonia wafting from the glass. Sipped it slowly. Enjoyed every drop.

Kintsugi

I'm a little teapot, short and stout.
Here is my handle, here is my spout.
When I get all steamed up, hear me shout-

Kintsugi
is the Japanese art
of repairing broken pottery with liquid gold.

Well whoever put me back together
cheaped the fuck out.

My cracks are sealed with lead.
Dull gray metal flows through my porcelain skin like veins
or poison through them
and some of my more jagged
chips are still unfilled in

but at least I don't leak anymore.
The stuff of bullets holds me together.
So why don't you sip what I steep?
It's sweet as melted sugar
and it'll put you down like hemlock
if you wait long enough.

My medicine is unrealized alchemy.
Like a blackjack I am small but heavy and blunt
Breaking made me dangerous as well as beautiful.
Shattering is what showed me how to draw blood.

You wanna get burned?
Just tip me over and
pour me out.

Poetry Lessons

Every poem is a list poem if you read it often enough.//
Every poem is an erasure if you edit hard enough.//
Every poem is a love poem if you care enough.//
Every poem is a breakup poem if it's not enough.//
Every poem is a persona poem if you're honest enough.//
Every poem is a form poem if you study it close enough.//
Every poem is an epistle if you put it in a bottle.//
Every poem is a novel if it cares enough.//
Every poem is a prayer if you repeat it enough.//
Every breath is a poem if you repeat it.//
Is a prayer if you repeat it.//
Is a miracle if you are enough.//
Which you are

Someday I'll Love Troy Cunio

after Frank O'Hara /
after Roger Reeves /
after Ocean Vuong

And that day was yesterday.
Remember? They watched
themselves wax & wane,
felt their veins
beating like the waves at high tide.
They huddled together
against the rain. They tried
not to mention thirst. Everyone
is a subway station.
No one is anything but under
construction.
Look at all they built, one scar
at a time.
Look at how they crossed the waters.
The conflagration
has spread from the bridge
and the whole city is alight.
From the rubble, watch them begin again.
They only need your body.
It doesn't matter which one.

speed

morning

shadows on the interstate
        sympathy growing
                heavy in my chest like
a tumor
        or a heart
and I am going to see my brother

who was a phantom of my childhood
        a homunculus in my booster seat
                who learned to talk by listening

to whispers of *that boy*
        just ain't

right
        in the fast lane
a car scrapes past
        dragging its bumper
a fiberglass ball and chain

        I want speed like that
my burdens leaving pebbles behind me

with sunshine bouncing off my mirrored retinas
        the fastest man in a fast land

the blacks of the billboard girl's eyes

        follow me

my asphalt bloodstream
        mirages

all the way to Miami

my mother told me don't
        buy your brother's breakfast
                my father had more work than
he could run from

I leadfoot into the glowing
        sizzling southbound
my excuses all have alibis

cold pizza and coffee

break bottles in my belly
        all the maybe I wills I haven't
in the back of my Chevy

like a spare tire

I don't know how to change

The Woman Whose Job It Was To Watch The Moon

They sat around the fire sipping pineneedle tea in the purple evening. The Milkman had folded his spidery legs onto a small tin bucket he'd found beside the shelter. Chickpea lotused on her mat. The others squatted or plopped down right on the dirt. Haiku's cigarillo sent a tiny column of smoke up through the clearing. A man they didn't know (he'd introduced himself as Smiley) slept in the shelter. He looked like a black slug wrapped in his garbage bag, snoring at odd intervals. Nobody spoke. The moon rose and became a mirror for the weary planet. It had been a long and rocky hike from Mosquito Pond.

Finally Swampfoot threw a stick in the fire and said, "There's a town down south pays a lady just to watch the moon."

"Really?" said Chickpea.

"That's hocky," said the Milkman, at the same time.

"No, it's true," put in Blackbeard. "I've been there."

Swampfoot looked at him.

"About 50 years ago, I forget the name of the place, they had a really good mayor. He managed to scrape together a budget surplus and so he spent a solid week pondering how best to spend it. All that money was going to waste just sitting there, not serving the townsfolk. The mayor couldn't sleep because of that thought. He stayed up pacing his study all night. His wife tried to slip sleep medicine into his coffee but he smelled it and threw it out."

"Doesn't seem too smart to me. Nyquil's not bad if you mix it right," interrupted the Milkman.

Blackbeard narrowed his eyes. The fire shined off his chin. "Hush. Let her tell the story."

"One night the moon was full and it shined through the mayor's window. He stopped his restless pacing and watched it. He went down into the street and walked the empty thoroughfares of his town watching it cross the empty sky.

When the sun rose it occurred to him that some nights the moon might not be seen by anyone. It was so graceful but sometimes, maybe nobody noticed it. It might go all the way from horizon to horizon with no one to appreciate it. It might even spin, or jump, or cry- no one would know.

The mayor decided right then that the extra money would hire someone to watch the moon. That very morning he ordered the town clocktower cleaned out and furnished with a comfortable bed, a telescope, and a desk."

Blackbeard put in, "I heard it was falling down. They had to renovate and rebuild the whole place."

"That's right," said Swampfoot. "Took a year. Meanwhile, the mayor spent every night except dark moons walking the streets with it. One night he came across a homeless woman. She was sitting on her cardboard staring up at the moon. The search to fill the job opening was going poorly- that's why the mayor was so restless. But as soon as he saw her he knew immediately that she was the one. Her name was Amaris."

"Fitting," remarked Chickpea. She had been listening carefully. This was the sort of story she liked.

"The mayor thought so, too," continued Swampfoot, but before she could go on the Milkman snorted.

"All kinds of things get changed to make a better story."

"Not this one." Swampfoot's voice took on an edge. "Tell him, Blackbeard, if you've really been there."

"It's true. There's a statue with a plaque and everything."

"Anyway, Amaris moved to the clocktower the next morning. Her responsibilities were simple- every night except dark moons, she was to watch it until dawn. If it was cloudy or foggy and the moon hidden, she had to note this before she could go to sleep. She normally stayed up though, just in case. She didn't have to do anything else- write, work, speak to people, nothing.

By day Amaris would go to bookstores and coffeeshops and restaurants she couldn't afford when she was on the streets. She'd sleep in the afternoons. By night she watched. Full moons. Half moons. Fingernail- thin crescents. Murky moons barely visible. Red warrior moons like wide eyes peeking over the hills. And her favorites, the bright moons so radiant she could see herself in them. Years passed and she had a daughter. Named her Luna, of course.

Amaris eventually became so attuned to the moon that her blood began to have its own tides. One month her body waxed until it was almost too large for the little room in the clocktower, then waned into almost nothing. This continued every month until she disappeared for good. Luna took over the job and she still does it. She's probably up tonight, staring at the same moon we are."

They sat there like that in the silver glow. Even the Milkman didn't say anything. In fact, he was almost asleep- the fire had lulled him into a kind of bored tranquility. His cigarette had gone out some minutes before. Haiku still hadn't said anything, either- he was smoking and thinking about Satori. In a week it would be his birthday. Chickpea had moved into shavasana and it was hard to tell if she was still on earth or not. After a minute Blackbeard spoke up.

"You know, there's more. I met Luna once when I was there. The town's called Stawford. There's nothing else interesting about it. Well Luna's getting on in years herself, but she has no child to take over for her when she starts to wax and wane like her mother did. And not for lack of trying. Her firstborn hated the moon, so he stared at the sun just to spite her. He went blind and walked off a bridge. And then her daughter was the opposite. She liked making eyes at the moon so much at that some folks said she was in love with it- and maybe she was. Her eyes got big as an owls, and sure enough one night she up and flew away. I don't know if that's true or not but that's what Luna told me. Strange woman, but a good sort."

The fire eased down to coals and as the night coldened, one by one they rose. Swampfoot, Chickpea and Blackbeard bundled into the shelter with Smiley (still snoring gently and rustling in his bag). Milkman shook his head and breathed out steam before going to unzip his tent. Haiku was the last to go. When the chill became too much for him he went off into the woods where his hammock was hung. The pines were tall and thin, and despite his quilt Haiku shivered the whole night through.

we suburban beatniks
we plastic punks
        we have done everything
                been everywhere
                met everyone
        and after all there's no one
                to share it with

                                            no one at all

32 Bullet Points That Have Been Mistaken for a Handgun

- a wallet
2. raised hands
- a book
- the inside of a book
- a Qur'an
- the insides of the Qur'an
- what's inside of a wallet
- or what's not
- the back of a head
- childhood
- a cell phone in a bank robbers

12s. of #s
- the start of a race
- race
- a supersoaker
- skittles/sweet tea

17. years old
18. old
19. 94, Notorious B.I.G.'s album *Ready To Die.*
- please don't shoot
- the dance beat in every surviving gay bar in my city
- calming down an autistic kid
- stop and frisk
- stop
- frisking
- a metaphor
- a pointing finger
- on the post or play button
- right clicks
- an itchy one-grip

(3)1. in the chamber
32. in the clip

When we are angels

for A. I.

our connection is deeper than friendship
                               love
                               blood
We are simply the same light
shining through different bodies
                               facets of God-In-The-World

You, a
thirtysomething-Italian-American-wanderer-poetess-yogi-lesbian-writerofbullshitformoney-ghost-unbearableangel
Me, a
twentysomething-Italian-American-wanderer-poet-straight-writerofbullshitforfacebooklikes-ghost-unbearableangel

When you tell the wires holding the the world together
that you are killing yourself,
I think of the time you told me it was okay
to be healthy and an artist.

I imagine you grooming your wings whenever I drink alone.

Once, I saw you spread yourself thin over a page
                               over a stage
         strip until you were clothed with only silky
            violence
            violin
         light small fires on your body until I could smell
            your fingerprints burning.

Then you wrote me a story about how to look at overcast
    skies and see peace
              satori
              a wise woman
       gave me the smashed fishbowl your old house
          had been in until you grew strong
          enough to hold a hammer
       invited me out for drinks as if you hadn't just
          changed literature forever

I put you in my backpack when I left our city forever
                                a few months
  pass you around to the people I meet, hoping they are
      one of us.
  write you on postcards and send them to strangers
  think about you, unmoored on America's asphalt ocean

 pray that you are happy

      that when you look to the clouds,

you still see the same faces in them
you taught me to look for

[sometimes it rains]

Lakeland Blues Traveler

I'd spent most of the night on a Lakeland front porch drinking wine and watching Florida Southern College coeds stumble back home beneath the spreading oaks. The morning woke me still hazy and when I got somewhat cleaned up and Advil'd up and driving, Gillian Welch's voice convinced me to take a scenic route back to I-4, by which I mean I got so distracted singing along that I forgot where I was. *Oh me oh my oh, look at Miss Ohio, she's runnin around with her ragtop down. I wanna do right, just not right now.* Following the signs and one way streets that all seemed to lead to nowhere in particular, I came across a park across the street from a row of rotting abandoned houses. A couple sat on a truckbed by the street, watching the clouds go by.

He had on a Hawaiian shirt, open to show off his Italian chest. Bright and hairy as a billboard. She had more crystals on her than a geode does in it. But it was the nylon and wood on her lap that caught my eye. I always try to notice things that are alive. Things that can sing. I stopped my Chevy.

Rather, I drove past them, changed my mind, pulled into a spot reserved for disabled veterans, had a fit of guiltiness, pulled out of said spot, parked on the street, got out, popped the trunk, siezed my steel-string by the neck, and walked up towards the pair. They stared at me like I had just gotten 2 hours of sleep and was still visibly tipsy.

Oh, you've got an ax, she said.

Her name was Basha and he was Tony. She was a travelling musician, he was a sound tech. He was a real listener- the only things that came out of his mouth were his name and his cigarette. They're trying to start a recording studio in Lakeland. That Laketown Sound, Basha called it. We're gonna show the world.

We played a few songs together- she had a soulful kind of phrasing, like Aretha Franklin singing Woodie Guthrie tunes. She sang "Proud Mary" like it was a love song. A really funky love song. Big wheels turning under her fingertips. Tony rocking back and forth like the rhythm. She played a classical- fingerstyle, like me only smoother- and she wore a mini-speaker on her hip so her quiet croons echoed across the retention pond. She adjusted the quartz on her forehead so the microphone headset would sit just right. Expanding her energy one way or another.

I sat on the tailgate of her station wagon- the truck alongside belonged to Tony- and she told me how she'd driven it down from Detroit trading songs for gasoline. How she'd slept in the back with her guitar case for a pillow. She asked me for an original. I said I don't have any. That's okay, she said. When you play anything, you make it yours. You make it an original. A couple more folks stopped and listened as I crowed an old song I'd learned the night before. *Rye whiskey, rye whiskey, rye whiskey I cry, if a tree don't fall on me, I'll live till I die.*

I only had an hour till a friend was supposed to capture my soul on an SD card back in Orlando, so I stood to get on the road. Basha said a prayer over me and hummed a long mournful ohm while I prayed silently to Jesus that her intentions be stronger than her aura. Either way she was powerful- for a minute the flat Florida swampland resonated with a sound like the Himalayas. As I closed the door and drove off she hollered, You stay strong, boy. You got the fire. Off I went, sober at last but higher than ever, in search of the interstate and a place where I could burn. And I burned.

If Books Could Kill

In April 2016 the University of Central Florida library was evacuated by law enforcement after a student reported a "Middle Eastern gunman" in the stairwell. He had "mistaken" her Qu'ran for a weapon. This poem is in his voice.

I know what I saw.
I heard her prayers. They were veiled
so I knew her chants were bullets. Nothing else
is so automatic, so sincere. The sura was a slide racking,
a shot fired skywards as if God were a bullseye.

I realized that this library was an armory.
She might has well have been reading
from the magazine of an AK-47.
I tried to throw the books at her,
but they were already pointed at me.

There is no reason
for a private citizen to own a Vladimir Nabokov
or Amiri Baraka. Or a Q'uran.
Even a name can be a weapon if it is sharp enough.
That's why I advocate for pun control.
Only the police and military should have access to weapons of mass instruction.
We must teach our children to aim as young as possible
and not to play with loaded language.

How else will we make America hate again?

When English ceased to be the only language of America,
I too felt free to speak without translation.

Violence is my mother tongue.

When I say Bible, it means buckshot.
When i say op-ed, it means car bomb.
Terrorist and illegal are synonyms for brown.

So maybe I wasn't speaking literally
when I called the cops. Call it poetic
justice. I said pistol,
knowing they'd bring them.
I wasn't lying. I was prophesying.
Soon there were weapons in the stairwell
and the prayers had moved outside.

I called in the big guns because some things
cannot be solved by argument. Bolt actions speak louder
than words. Shotguns can breach any subject
as easily as a locked door. If you're trying to make a point,
a hollowpoint is the most penetrating.

But even if our lexicon crosses out all others,
all moral reservations buried like a hatchet,
all opposition hanged like teaching children to spell,
the histories will still be written.
All our victories are Pyrrhic in the face of memory.
Even if we erase everyone not white enough
to put in an blank journal,
some of the survivors may scrawl
consciences on their skin.

Dictionaries will always be thick enough to stop a bullet.
Revolutions are not always bloody enough to murder.

If books could kill
that woman in the stairwell
would be a lot less dangerous.

An Academic Poem

for Billy Collins

You write a poem about birds, and through it all
you never bother to get out of bed.

You write a poem about the beach at night,
and it's only a metaphor for poetry.
        Billy, nobody wants to watch you masturbate.

You write a poem about horses,
you even name a book after it,
but it's only about a picture of horses
watching you as you eat dinner with your wife.

You even manage to make love
an exercise in mildness.

You write a poem about sitting at your window.
And another.
And another.
You say all the poets in the world are doing the same,
but not all the poets in the world are clones of you.

Yes, you and I
are somewhat alike.
We studied the same thing in college.
We're both white men trying to have something to say.
The difference is I refuse to pretend that all poets
are like you and me.
The day I see you at a slam,
when you lose to a teenage aspiring rapper
who does not identify on the gender binary,
I will apologize, shake your hand,

tear up this poem, and buy all your books
to make up for stealing them from the internet.

You write poems the way most people write shopping lists,
dreary litanies of ennui and comfort.
Billy, even you cannot romanticize suburbia.
Just because you watch us from your plush square cage,
in some carefully manicured and gated mortgage factory,
do not imagine that we are not poets. We are literary
pirates raiding the world for booty.
We are cowboys singing songs as
we ride across the vast prairie of loneliness. We write
on buses and interstates
and in the lulls between failed relationships.
We read through our headphones. We write drunk
and edit drunk and recite drunk and weep sober.
Billy, when was the last time you were drunk?
When was the last time you wept?

Your iceberg theory has sunk you.
Your poems beg for analysis, crying
"come read us, our simplicity is deceptive, we promise."
Your poems are bland billboards for a veterinarian's office,
or a divorce lawyer.
You depend on the critics to give your poems meaning.
You depend on advertisements to give your poems
        meaning.

When our poems want to be analyzed,
        they go to a therapist.
When our poems want to be criticized,
        they get a significant other.

Billy, us gutter poets live in the same city
that you do, but a different planet.
We gather in bars to drink in cheap verses
as if they were beer, or milk.
Our lips, loose with liquor,
flap like wounded birds until the morning.
We speak the easy metaphors because we made bets
on who can work the most instances of the word "booty"
into their poems.
We are punslingers.
We dare make the stupid jokes,
and we dare to laugh at them.

This poem is a bare booty clapping in your face-
you are too old
and nearsighted to watch or be aroused,
but I pray you will smell the musk.
We may write badly, but we write
about the important things.
We are in the streets. We are in punk shows. Hip hop
shows. Minimum wage jobs. DIY art openings. Drunk tanks.
Parties. Protests. Liquor stores. Church.
We brush the dust from our shoulders as we stare hazily
at the stars. We live on black coffee and barely contained
manic dread. We wear obscurity like homemade jewelry.
We couldn't sell out if we wanted to.

The word on the zine is,
these days you are too literary to even teach.

Billy, I know your brow is up in a spotless tower somewhere
and you wouldn't dream of sullying your pen with a cliche,

so I'll say it for you. Listen up.

This town ain't big enough for the two of us.

Botflies

worms in my skin

squirmy bulbous things
gorged on muscle and tissue

suffocate them
with fresh linens and tape
feel them move, gentle hornet-stings like an infant's kick

feel them dance as I make love
don't tell her what's under the bandage-
a necrotic feast,

my Geigerian pregnancy

quintuplets

craterous supplemental nostrils

constellation of decay and gestation

***

this other jungle, suburban, brutal. SUVs eye sidewalks hungrily

advertisements howling like monkeys. throwing shit

invisible serpentine waveforms gather their venom

a clean waiting room, blonde haired televisions explaining the importance of moisture, of recognizing symptoms, of attractive insurance rates

starched white walls, overcoats

my flesh pumped with salt water and lidocaine

curved tweezers like a bird's cruel beak

the numb tugging of the blades
a single brown droplet on the surgeon's mask

the miracle of parasites

aborted with two hours of a scalpel
shaped like a tiny cookie cutter

larvae in a bottle on a table framed by blood and paper

a week's worth of pills all at once, to be sure

the cool wind in my stitches

Guate Nocturne

Here, the night is the silky green of desperate progress
        reckless and thick
The obscenity that is abundance trickles down slow
        as petroleum from the north
Here all the good things sleep behind steel doors
        and shotguns

In another part of the city, children scrape survival
        off of discarded plates and to-go boxes
In another part, sordid acts between pale bodies in a row
        of rickety iron bunks
In another part, a man scrubs a bus the color of blood,
        pointlessly. The windows left jagged as a warning
The morning will bring newspapers singing distant gunfire,
        rape, fiery auto collisions
The day will cast this vermillion glow grey- here, only its
        own light can veil this city beautiful
Coffee, dark and murderous, will propel me back home
        and so I sleep
Wrapped in my smoggy bed, dreaming of taxis
        and small twisted gods.

A waning the color of mercury drips through and glints
        on the barbed wire
In another part of the country, a serpent spreads its wings.

the boy or girl

across the room, glowing softly, fading

if they would disrobe, outstretch, the walls
       would melt like fondue

if they would speak, the music would stop
       until they finished, and longer

if they would get off their phone, in that
       moment an old friend or lover
       would call me again

if they would look up, meet my eye,
       God might just look down
       for the first time this millenium

I wonder if they know that a lightbulb lingers
       on your vision if you stare as it
       flickers out

I wonder if they know quasars do the same thing
that collapse is not the letdown, but the promise

that even the Rockies burn inside

even the Pacific does, down in its steamy
       unbright bowels

even I do, small and plumping and quiet

maybe they have a piercing in their eyebrow or nose,
       or maybe it's just their bones, gleaming

Juice is based on an ostensibly true news report of a woman whose DUI was dismissed after it was determined that her body metabolized all sugars into alcohol.

Someday I'll Love Troy Cunio is a response to Frank O'Hara's *Katy*, Roger Reeves's *Someday I'll Love Roger Reeves*, and Ocean Vuong's *Somedeay I'll Love Ocean Vuong*. With thanks to Hanif Willis-Abdurraqib. You should consider writing your own version as an exercise in self-love.

32 Bullet Points That Have Been Mistaken for a Handgun remembers Amadou Diallo, Philando Castile, Charles Kinsey, the library scare at UCF, Trayvon Martin, the Orlando 49, Christopher Wallace, and countless other people and incidents. With thanks to Jay Ward.

Lakeland Blues Traveler really happened, but I haven't heard from Basha or Laketown Sound since.

A rough draft of *If Books Could Kill* was featured on the PARKXVI youtube channel.

Billy Collins, if you ever read *An Academic Poem*, I stand by it. I know you're busy what with reading on NPR every other weekend, but seriously dude. Get out of the house every once in a while. Also, you're boring.

Botflies is a completely true poem. I have five purple scars on my arm to this day.

Guate Nocturne was published in *Revista Literaria Centroamericana* along with a Spanish translation by Gabriel Setright that is a much better poem than the original.

Also by Troy Kody Cunio:

Love Poems to Anyone- short chapbook of poetry
The Adventures of Pop Punk Donald Trump- echapboook
run away enough times to know it won't solve anything-
    short chapbook of prose memoirs
Little Lost Poems vols 1-3- small stones

Made in the USA
Charleston, SC
23 December 2016